BILL GATES

LEGENDS AND LEGACIES

THE BIOGRAPHY OF
BILL GATES

Published by
Rupa Publications India Pvt. Ltd 2024
7/16, Ansari Road, Daryaganj
New Delhi 110002

Sales centres:
Bengaluru Chennai
Hyderabad Jaipur Kathmandu
Kolkata Mumbai Prayagraj

Copyright © Rupa Publications India Pvt. Ltd 2024

The views and opinions expressed in this book are the author's own and the facts are as reported by him which have been verified to the extent possible, and the publishers are not in any way liable for the same.

All rights reserved.
No part of this publication may be reproduced, transmitted, or stored in a retrieval system, in any form or by any means, electronic, mechanical, photocopying, recording or otherwise, without the prior permission of the publisher.

P-ISBN: 978-93-6156-127-6
E-ISBN: 978-93-6156-392-8

First impression 2024

10 9 8 7 6 5 4 3 2 1

Printed in India

This book is sold subject to the condition that it shall not, by way of trade or otherwise, be lent, resold, hired out, or otherwise circulated, without the publisher's prior consent, in any form of binding or cover other than that in which it is published.

Contents

Introduction	7
William Henry Gates III : The Early Years	9
Harvard's Most Successful Dropout	16
Byte by Byte	26
Hits and Misses	35
Window(s) to Success	45
The Next Chapter in Tech	59
The Stumbling Blocks	68
'To Whom Much Is Given, Much Is Expected'	77

Introduction

Hey there, curious minds!

Have you ever wondered how a boy with a curious mind and a passion for computers grew up to change the world? Let me introduce you to William Henry Gates III, better known as Bill Gates, the man who turned a childhood curiosity into a technological revolution. He didn't have a cape or superpowers, but his vision and determination reshaped the digital landscape and brought computers into homes and offices around the globe.

Imagine growing up in Seattle, Washington, in a home buzzing with the excitement of new ideas and intellectual debates. Bill was born on October 28, 1955, into a family that valued education and hard work. His father, William Gates Sr., was a prominent lawyer, and his mother, Mary, was a dedicated teacher, community activist, and businesswoman. Bill, the second of three children, enjoyed a nurturing environment that encouraged competition and curiosity.

As a child, Bill wasn't your typical team player. He preferred individual activities like roller skating, tennis, and water skiing. His family, rooted in Protestant values, fostered a spirit of competition that stayed with him throughout his life. It didn't matter whether it was a game of hearts or a swim to the dock—there was always a reward for winning and a penalty for losing. This competitive spirit, along with his insatiable curiosity, shaped his future.

Despite his loving family, young Bill sometimes worried his parents with his aloofness and penchant for getting into trouble at school. They sought help from a counselor who advised them to channel his energies positively. Bill's life took a turn for the better when he joined the Boy Scouts, earning his Eagle Scout badge, and developed a love for reading, especially science fiction.

At thirteen, Bill's life took a significant turn when he enrolled at the Lakeside School in Seattle. Here, he met Paul Allen, who shared his fascination with computers. The school's Mother's Club had purchased a teletype terminal, giving students access to a computer—a rarity in those days. Bill was instantly captivated, spending endless hours in the computer room. His passion for computers was born, and there was no looking back.

Together with Paul, Bill delved into programming, developing games and software like Tic-Tac-Toe and Traf-O-Data. Their enthusiasm even led them to hack into a Computer Centre Corporation computer to gain extra time on it, earning them a reprimand but also fueling their drive to innovate.

Bill's early influences were not just limited to his family. His father taught him the importance of balancing diverse interests with family commitments and community service. His mother, along with his maternal grandmother, inspired him to do more for others. One of his earliest teachers, Mrs. Blanche Caffiere, a librarian at View Ridge Elementary School, played a crucial role in nurturing his love for books and learning.

After graduating from Lakeside, Bill attended Harvard University, where he continued to pursue his passion for computers. Along with Paul Allen, Bill founded Microsoft, a company that would revolutionize the computer industry.

Bill Gates' journey continues to inspire millions, reminding us that with the right mindset and dedication, we too can change the world.

So, dear explorers, take a page from Bill Gates' book—stay curious, embrace challenges, and never stop learning. Who knows? The next big idea might just be waiting for you to discover.

1

William Henry Gates III : The Early Years

> Success is a lousy teacher. It seduces smart people into thinking they can't lose.
>
> —*Bill Gates*

William Henry Gates III was born in Seattle, Washington, on 28 October 1955. His father, William Gates Sr., was a prominent lawyer, and his mother, Mary, was a teacher, community activist and businesswoman. Bill was the second child in the family after his sister Kristianne (Kristi), who was one year older than him. He has another sister, Libby, who is nine years younger. The Gates family were important members of the local Protestant community. Conscious of her duties as a mother, Mary had quit her teaching job earlier, devoting her time mainly to raising family.

Overall, it was a happy and loving family, devoted to Christian values, and caring and supportive of one another. As a child, Bill especially enjoyed non-team events liked roller skating, and later as he grew up, tennis and water

Bill Gates
Credits: Kjetil Ree, CC BY-SA 3.0 <https://creativecommons.org/licenses/by-sa/3.0>, via Wikimedia Commons

skiing. Given their Protestant background, the family encouraged competition—a trait that would stay with Gates for the rest of his life. 'It didn't matter whether it was hearts or pickle ball, or swimming to the dock… there was always a reward for winning, and there was always a penalty for losing,' once a visitor to the family noted.

> **Fun Fact**
> Innovative Work Culture: Gates fostered a competitive yet innovative work environment at Microsoft, encouraging employees to push the boundaries of software development and technological advancement.

However, despite all the love and care, certain aspects of Bill's behaviour had started causing concern among his parents as he was growing up. Without any apparent reason, he had begun to withdraw into a shell—becoming more and more quiet and aloof. Sometimes just to check, when his father would call and ask, 'What are you doing?' His reply would be, 'Thinking. Don't you ever think?'

He would be easily bored—and when bored, would need some change. At school he would often get into trouble with other children, and even talk back to his teachers. He was generally struggling in life. His parents had started getting worried about his behaviour and feared he might become a loner. His father decided to consult a counsellor. After a few

Seattle, Washington 1955 Yellow Book
Credits: Public Roads Administration - Federal Works Agency (predecessor to the United States Department of Transportation)., Public domain, via Wikimedia Commons

sessions, the counsellor too didn't sound too hopeful. He said to his father that there was no use trying to force him to conform. 'You're going to lose. You had better adjust.'

They thus sought to channelize his energies in positive productive directions. They made him participate in boy scout activities (he even earned his Eagle Scout badge) and also encouraged him to take part in team sports. They were happy to discover his growing interest in reading and so fuelled his curiosity further through science fiction books. These steps worked to improve matters and things began to change.

New School Helps Him to Blossom

When he was thirteen, Gates was admitted to an exclusive upscale Lakeside School in Seattle. Although his family was a supporter of the public education system, they felt this new school would challenge him and help him to blossom. And blossom he did! A certain turn of events here gave a new direction to his life, tapped into his hidden talents, and brought out the best in him. He met Paul Allen, two years his senior, and despite differences in personalities, struck a great friendship with him. What brought the two together was their love of computers. Being an intelligent child and good in math, he had developed an inclination towards the machine, which was quite a novelty those days. Here, the Mother's Club of the school had used proceeds from the school's rummage sale to buy a teletype terminal for students to have familiarity with the computer. Bill, being a natural in this environment, felt quite at home in the computer room. This was his calling. He would find it difficult to tear himself from the machine. He later wrote, 'There's something neat about

> **Fun Fact**
>
> Early Tech Prodigy: At 13, Bill Gates wrote his first computer program, marking the beginning of his journey into technology and innovation. This early achievement set the stage for his future groundbreaking work in the tech industry.

the machine... It was hard to tear myself away from a machine at which I could so unambiguously demonstrate success.' Both he and Paul had become quite passionate about computers.

Paul Allen would often dress up in a sports coat and a tie, and carry a leather briefcase, and bus it down to the local computer gurus' offices in search of discarded code. While codes would be easily available to the employees of the companies, Paul and Bill had to hunt for it. Allen would boost a smaller Bill into dumpsters and they would get 'these coffee-stained texts (of computer code) from behind the offices'. Once, they even found the printout of an important source code that unlocked a lot of secrets.

> **Fun Fact**
>
> Birth of Microsoft: In 1975, Bill Gates and Paul Allen co-founded Microsoft, a company that would become a cornerstone of the tech industry and revolutionize personal computing worldwide.

A result of these efforts was that around this time, Bill was able to develop a programme called Tic-Tac-Toe, in BASIC computer language, which allowed users to play games against the computer—and later, another one, Traf-O-Data, along with Paul, to make traffic counters based on an Intel 8008 processor. In their childish enthusiasm, once when they even hacked a Computer Centre Corporation computer to get extra time on it. They were reprimanded for it and also banned for four weeks from using the computer.

That's how life was when they were together at Lakeside. Soon, all this was about to change. As Paul was two years ahead of him, he left and went on to join Washington State University. Bill was to follow later. Life had too many surprises in store for them.

Early Influences

Children learn from their environment, especially from elders at home and school. Impressions and influences in formative years play a major role in later life. In case of Bill, this was particularly so, as he was fortunate to be guided by some very strong individuals, very rooted in their ethics and positive values.

Bill's father profoundly influenced his son, instilling in him lessons that deeply shaped his personality. He often imparted wisdom, emphasizing the importance of maintaining diverse interests and hobbies without neglecting family commitments. His father believed in showing solidarity with the community, whether through small acts like collecting funds for slum rehabilitation or helping a neighbor clear a storm-damaged driveway. He encouraged Bill to step out of his comfort zone and embrace new experiences, teaching him that failure brings valuable lessons that will be beneficial in the long run. Moreover, he advocated for a balanced life, combining indoor and outdoor activities, and blending classroom learning with practical experiences. His father also stressed the significance of curiosity and continuous learning. He often reminded Bill of the biblical lesson from the Book of Luke in the New Testament: "To whom much is given, much is expected," encouraging those with means to assist other's whenever possible.

Among Bill's earliest influences were some strong women as well, whose ideas and thoughts guided him from an early age. These include his mother and his maternal grandmother.

> **Fun Fact**
> Impact on Personal Computing: Gates' vision has significantly shaped modern operating systems and applications, revolutionizing the way people interact with technology and access information.

Young Bill Gates
Credits: (Dcoetzee) Albuquerque, New Mexico police department, Public domain, via Wikimedia Commons

Gates said in a Harvard commencement speech about his mother, *'She never stopped pressing me to do more for others.'* In this context, he has also talked of a letter his mother had written to his fiancée Melinda in 1993, a little before his marriage, where her

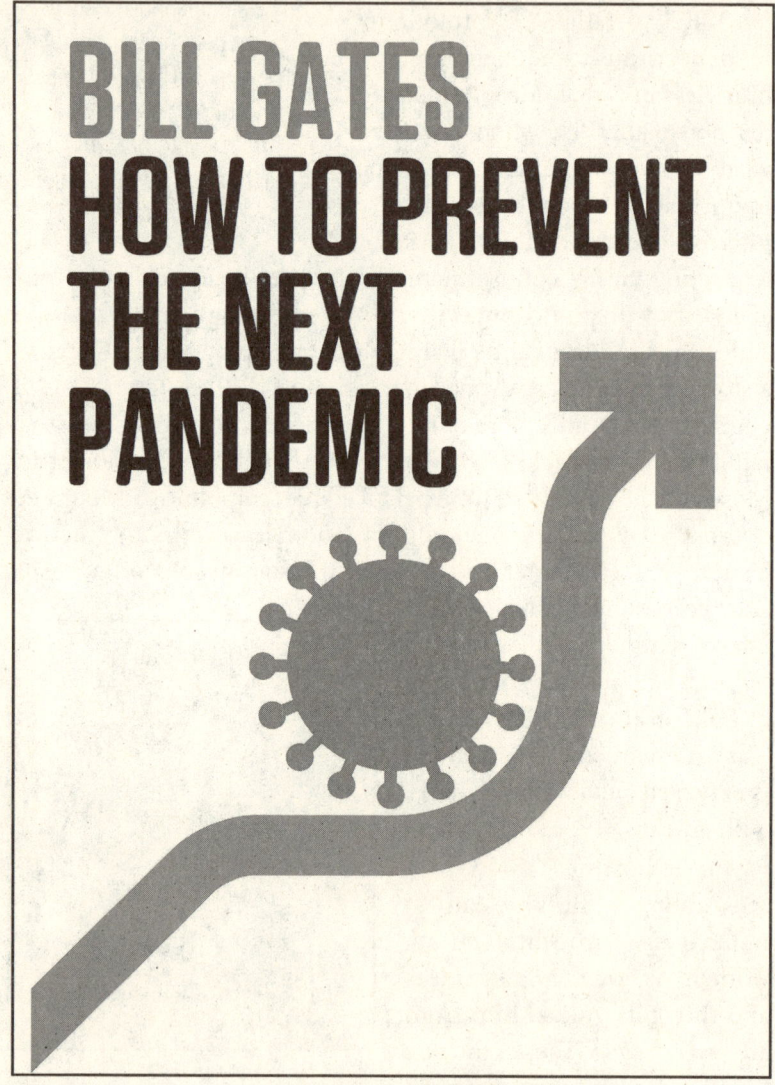

How to Prevent the Next Pandemic by Bill Gates

advice echoed Voltaire's belief that with great power comes great responsibility. We must recall that around this time, Gates was one of the wealthiest people in the world, and his mother expected him and his wife to do much for others.

Mrs Blanche Caffiere—Friend, Philosopher and Guide

Gates has also singled out one of his earliest teachers, Mrs Blanche Caffiere, a librarian in Seattle's View Ridge Elementary school, for special mention, as one who had a big influence on him. When he was a 'timid fourth grader,' she drew him out of his shell, and she, with her knowledge about books, fuelled his interest in different types of reading.

> **Fun Fact**
> Billionaire at 31: By the age of 31, Gates had achieved billionaire status, underscoring his exceptional business skills and the rapid ascent of Microsoft in the technology sector.

'Mrs Caffiere took me under her wing and helped make it okay for me to be a messy, nerdy boy, who was reading lots of books,' said Gates.

She would often start with questions like, 'What do you like to read?' and 'What are you interested in?' She gave him great biographies she had read. She would genuinely listen to what he had to say. 'Through those book conversations in the library and in the classroom, we became good friends,' said Gates.

Mrs Caffiere died in 2006, shortly after her 100th birthday. Before she passed away, Gates had an opportunity to thank her for the important role she had played in his life, '…stoking my passion for learning at a time when I easily could have gotten turned off by school.'

2

Harvard's Most Successful Dropout

> I failed in some subjects in (an) exam,
> but my friend passed in all. Now he's an engineer
> in Microsoft and I am the owner of Microsoft.
> —*Bill Gates*

Life at Harvard

For most people, getting into Harvard is a dream. It's the opening up of new avenues and opportunities. While for Gates too, it was not any different, he was looking for something beyond what Harvard had to offer. And given his determination and vision, it was to show up soon.

A math prodigy who was in love with computers, Gates was ready to paint a larger canvas of his own life at the time of leaving school. When he graduated from the Lakeside School in Seattle, he was a National Merit Scholar, having scored 1590 out of 1600 on the Scholastic Aptitude Tests (more commonly known as SATs) in 1973.

Given his exceptional school credits, his entry into Harvard in 1973 was rather easy, and there he

> **Fun Fact**
>
> Wealth and Influence: For many years, Gates held the title of the world's richest person, a testament to his monumental success, strategic vision, and global influence in technology and business.

not only opted for pre-law major, but also took mathematics and graduate-level computer science courses. Although he chose law, as his father was an eminent lawyer and the family was keen on his joining the profession, his interest lay elsewhere.

As computers were his first love, at Harvard too he was driven by programming and he used this opportunity to spend as much time as possible on the school's computers. 'I used to sit in a lot of classes that I hadn't even signed up for,' he later recalled in his 2007 Harvard Commencement Speech. Harvard was a 'phenomenal experience' for him. 'Academic life was fascinating,' he said. According to him, it was an extraordinary experience to be 'amidst so much of energy and intelligence… It could be exhilarating, intimidating, sometimes even discouraging, but always challenging. It was an amazing privilege and though I left early, I was transformed by my years at Harvard.'

At Harvard again, he was less in his classes and more in the computer room. Although Paul had left school two years before him, Gates had kept in touch. Without him, he felt a little handicapped and was keen that the two resume their collaborative projects. 'We were each other's soundboards,' Paul had said in an interview later. After leaving school, Paul had joined Washington University, but on Bill's persuasion he left after two years and joined Honeywell near Boston. Being near to each other, the two could now pursue their dreams together. Bill remembers, they would call big companies and ask for programming assignments, and their reply would be, 'You guys are just high-school kids…We do that work ourselves.'

> **Fun Fact**
> Efficiency Advocate: Gates prioritizes efficiency and effectiveness in both his business and philanthropic efforts, striving to maximize impact and achieve meaningful results.

MICROSOFT

William H. Gates
President

819 Two Park Central Tower, Albuquerque, NM 87108
(505) 256-3600

Microsoft Co-Founder, Bill Gates first business card
Credits:https://i.redd.it/e28lfw1qu7i11.jpg, CC BY-SA 4.0 <https://creativecommons.org/licenses/by-sa/4.0>, via Wikimedia Commons

Baby Steps in Business

On a frigid December afternoon, as Paul was crossing the Harvard Yard, he chanced upon the January 1975 edition of the electronics journal, *Popular Electronics*. It had a picture of the kit of Altair 8800, a new microcomputer, on the cover, with the caption: 'Project Breakthrough, World's first Microcomputer Kit to rival commercial models (save over $1,000).'

Paul grabbed the copy and ran to Bill and suggested to him that they develop a programme for this simple little machine. Altair 8800 was not the first microcomputer, but it was the first to catch people's imagination. Economically priced, it was a big draw among computer enthusiasts. The computer didn't look like much, just a rectangular box with several rows of tiny toggle switches across the front and no software, disk drive or keyboard. The buyer had to assemble it from a kit. As against the modern personal computer (PC) that has 8 million bytes today, it had just 256 bytes.

> **Fun Fact**
> Global Health Impact: The Gates Foundation's initiatives in global public health have saved millions of lives, particularly through efforts to combat infectious diseases and improve healthcare access in developing countries.

Ryutaro Hashimo and Bill Gates
Credits: Prime Minister's Office Homepage, CC BY 4.0 <https://creativecommons.org/licenses/by/4.0>, via Wikimedia Commons

This was to be their big project together, though they had been collaborating on software projects earlier. In fact, now, excited as Paul was by the prospect of 'adopting' the machine, he kept telling Bill, 'Let's start a company. Let's do it.' Commenting on the episode later, Bill had remarked, 'We realized the revolution might happen without us. After we saw the article, there was no question of where our life would focus.'

Micro Instrumentation and Telemetry Systems's (MITS) co-founder, Ed Roberts, had earlier told them, 'We are getting about ten letters a day from people... I'd tell them whoever writes it first, gets the job.' Subsequently, as they got the go-ahead on the project, their next challenge was how and where to write the programme as they didn't have an Altair 8800. Despite this handicap, they found a solution and decided to use the Harvard computers for the job. For the next six weeks, Gates was like a possessed man.

During this time, he almost lived at Harvard. Unmindful of rest, sleep or food, he got down to the job at a furious pace. Grabbing a meal here or there, he would take a nap in a corner or would even dose off on the keyboard. As Paul was at Honeywell nearby, he would come regularly to assist and contribute his bit. They even hired some other Harvard students to assist them in small jobs. Many bugs were fixed later.

Their programme was soon ready, but they didn't have the right machine to test it. They had no option but to give the maiden demonstration right at MITS. Finally, it was decided that Paul would go, as in appearance he looked mature enough to handle important projects. He flew to Albuquerque for the presentation. Destiny was as if favouring them. The programme worked perfectly on the company's machine and the company accepted their product. 'I called Bill, and said it worked,' says Paul. 'We were over the moon.' Paul celebrated the success by treating himself to an extra large pizza. As their product was accepted, it resulted in a deal with the company, which agreed to distribute the machine as Altair BASIC, virtually accepting their imprint on it.

> **Fun Fact**
>
> Leadership Inspiration: Gates' leadership style and innovative thinking have inspired countless entrepreneurs, demonstrating the importance of vision, determination, and strategic planning.

Paul was offered a job at the company, which he accepted. Gates took leave of absence from Harvard, telling his parents that he would go back if things didn't work out. This first major break had boosted their confidence and they decided to form a company, though their foray into business was far from easy. Both he and Paul Allen spent a lot of time questioning themselves and their decision to risk everything and chase their dream. Perhaps destiny was nudging them towards this path as, around this time, an exciting opportunity presented itself before them.

They named their venture 'Micro-Soft' (a combination of 'microcomputer' and 'software') and continued to work under the aegis of MITS. However, within a year, towards the end of 1976, they became independent of MITS. The hyphen was dropped, and on 26 November 1976, the trade name 'Microsoft' was registered in New Mexico in the United States.

As their company began to grow, Gates felt no reason to go back to Harvard to get his degree. From now on, they continued to develop programming software for a variety of systems and companies. Later, on 1 January 1979, they moved their headquarters to Bellevue, Washington

Aerial view of Microsoft's West Campus, Redmond, WA, August 2009. Taken from 1,500 feet, looking southeast. The campus is bordered by 148th Ave to the west, SR 520 to the east, and 40th St. to the north
Credits: Jelson25, Public domain, via Wikimedia Commons

IBM Deal—the Turning Point

Some people called it the 'Deal of the Century.' And others, 'Deal with the Devil.'

Although, given his intelligence and drive, Gates was sure to be successful in his endeavours sooner or later, at this time, destiny appeared to be favouring him. The Altair success had brought them some basic recognition and had started getting them other assignments, but it was the International Business Machines Corporation (or as it is more popularly known—IBM) deal that was to be the biggest breakthrough of it all. It happened five years after their launching of Microsoft.

> **Fun Fact**
> Philanthropic Powerhouse: Co-founding the Bill & Melinda Gates Foundation, Gates significantly impacted global wellness, education, and poverty alleviation, creating one of the largest private charitable organizations in the world.

At the time of the IBM deal, Microsoft was a five-year-old company, run by two very young entrepreneurs. In the summer of 1980, Gates was just twenty-four and Paul had turned twenty-seven. As Gates looked younger than his age, people in the professional world often got confused about his exact role and position. There goes a story that once a member of the negotiating team took him to be a secretary and asked him to get coffee. That apart, the MITS connection had given them some basic recognition and they had started getting programming contracts for different companies.

Around this time, many computer companies—both established and start-ups—had begun to toy with the idea of producing smaller computers for the personal use of individuals. IBM remained the Big Blue, the colossus dominating the entire computer landscape. And as the buzz in favour of the smaller computers had started growing, IBM didn't want to lose out on the opportunity. It created a separate division for the development of PCs. In the summer of 1980, the company had developed a system, IBM PC, for which they needed an operating system (O/S). By some oversight, in IBM's 'briefing books,' Microsoft was listed as a major developer of O/S, so IBM decided to try them out and requested for an O/S for their new PC.

> **Fun Fact**
> Educational Investments: The Gates Foundation's contributions to education have notably improved educational outcomes, particularly in underserved communities, and supported innovative teaching and learning practices.

As the description of 'major developer of operating system' didn't quite fit their venture, Gates was a little surprised by the request. Gates's mother knew John Opel of IBM, who had served with her on the same board of United Way Charity (UWC) of America, and Microsoft was hoping to sell BASIC and other languages with the new IBM microcomputer. When this request for an O/S came from IBM, Gates was quite confused to say the least. Gary Kildall of Intergalactic Digital Research (IDR), who was an established figure in the field of microcomputers, had written the Control Program for Microcomputers (more commonly known as CP/M), a mass-market O/S that was ideally suited for the IBM PC. So, Gates referred the IBM people to him.

> **Fun Fact**
> Champion of Vaccines: Through his foundation, Gates has invested billions in global healthcare, particularly focusing on the development and distribution of vaccines to combat Contagious diseases, improving countless of lives.

Somehow things didn't go well between IBM and IDR. There are different versions about it—it's said that Kildall's wife was rather standoffish, and by the time the IBM team arrived at his residence, Kildall had gone away for his morning air-trip in his plane. Another story says that he did arrive around lunch time, but instead of an outright sale, Kildall asked for $10 per copy. In short, the negotiations didn't work out. Following these developments, Gates decided to explore other options as he didn't want to lose out on the other business he was hoping to get from IBM. He promised IBM an O/S.

There's a certain background as to how and why Gates promised IBM the O/S. Actually, Paul knew one Tim Patterson at Seattle Computer Products (SCP) who had been working on an alternative version of CP/M—he called it QDOS (short for Quick and Dirty O/S). Microsoft suggested to IBM that they

> **Fun Fact**
>
> Renowned Speaker: Gates is a highly sought-after speaker on topics ranging from technology and business to philanthropy, sharing his insights and experiences with diverse audiences around the world.

could buy this software and further work on it to suit the IBM PC. As they agreed to it, after the signing of the contract with IBM, Microsoft bought the software from SCP. Gates and Allen worked on it to suit the IBM requirement. It was approved, and finally the product was ready for shipping towards the end of 1981. The PC was to be named IBM PC-DOS.

Now, we have a twist in the tale. Although it appeared to be a regular deal, it turned out to be much more for Microsoft in the long run. Besides being a gifted software talent, Gates also had a shrewd business sense. It's said that perhaps Gates Sr.'s years of drafting contracts for companies also came in handy here. In the contract with IBM, a clause was cleverly added that allowed the company to sell the same O/S to other companies too under the name MS-DOS (short for Microsoft Disk O/S). It was this one line that changed the course of the entire computer industry and made Gates and Allen the richest people in the world. In addition to a licence fee per IBM machine, Microsoft was free to sell the same O/S to other manufacturers.

In the words of Bill Gates, around that time, the companies didn't think much of the software. In many cases, it came free with the equipment. For most, hardware was the thing. Gates said that the companies didn't realize that eventually software would be bigger than hardware. It was this mindset at the time due to which IBM didn't pay much heed to the seemingly 'harmless' clause. However, it set off a chain reaction that helped in revolutionizing the IT industry and bringing the computer into every home.

The IBM PC was the first major PC to hit the market, and as its popularity increased, competition was quick to take notice of the development and keen to take advantage of the situation. For a host of companies, it could be a gold mine—they started on the reverse engineering and were soon ready with an IBM clone. Now, as they wanted an O/S for it, Microsoft was quick at hand to supply one. It's reported that Compaq was the first to reverse-engineer the PC. Established in 1982, during its second year of operation, it was able to sell 53,000 PCs, hitting a sale of $111 million. In 1987, it hit the $1 billion mark, taking the shortest time to reach there. Then there were companies like Dell, Hewlett-Packard and others. Demand from all these had begun to add to Microsoft's sale.

Mr. Bill Gates and other dignitaries, at the Innovation Summit in COP 21, in Paris, France on November 30, 2015
Credits: Prime Minister's Office (GODL-India), GODL-India <https://data.gov.in/sites/default/files/Gazette_Notification_OGDL.pdf>, via Wikimedia Commons

In retrospect, after the IBM deal, there was no looking back for Microsoft. The IBM connection gradually propelled them into the big league and big money. If Microsft's revenue was $16,005 in 1976, in a short span of seven years it had grown to $55 million in 1983, and it stands at $125.8 billion as of June 2019. In over four decades of its existence, the company has traversed an interesting and long journey—it has had its share of ups and downs, and successes and failures, but overall, has continued to show a great degree of resilience and generally delivering better-than-expected results. What has made it a formidable market player and a dominant tech force needs closer analysis and scrutiny.

But first, some glimpses into the background conditions of the world and computer industry then, which made all this possible.

3

Byte by Byte

> Life is not fair, get used to it. We all need people who will give us feedback. That's how we improve.
> —Bill Gates

Growth of the Computer Industry and the Arrival of the Internet

After the Industrial Revolution of the 17th–18th centuries, the world had grown on the back of traditional manufacturing and service industries. So the rich list of the world contained names who owned tangible assets—real estate, factories, superstores, etc. But with the convergence of technologies, the world had started to become a different place and, in time, was set to undergo a paradigm shift. In our context here, since the issue is connected with the growth of the IT industry and the life of Bill Gates, the subject calls for a detailed analysis. Let's have a closer look.

After 1950, the world was set to be transformed on account of many major factors. First of all, owing to large-scale devastation during the World War II and the end of colonial rule, large parts of the world needed to be rebuilt. This had spurred industrial and manufacturing activity in the West, and especially in the US, on

> **Fun Fact**
>
> Eradicating Polio: Gates has been a key figure in the global effort to eradicate polio, dedicating substantial resources and advocacy to eliminate this debilitating disease worldwide.

an unprecedented scale. Secondly, after the fall of the Berlin Wall in 1989, the world had started to become a smaller place with markets opening up all over. And finally, with some major advances in the previous years, the computer industry had taken a few quantum leaps, and was set to become the dominant technology of the future. So, after the 1980s, all these factors combined together were going to make the world a very different

The Co-Chairman of the Bill and Melinda Gates Foundation, Mr. Bill Gates calling on the Prime Minister, Dr. Manmohan Singh, in New Delhi on July 25, 2009
Credits: Prime Minister's Office (GODL-India), GODL-India <https://data.gov.in/sites/default/files/Gazette_Notification_OGDL.pdf>, via Wikimedia Commons

place and even redefine the way modern empires would be built and fortunes made.

To understand how such events had begun to impact and change the lives of individuals and entities, let's first have a look at the history of computers, discover how it has evolved over time, and how things stood in this respect around 1950. Interestingly, some of the greatest inventions in history have been the result of trying circumstances, especially wars. In recent times, the World Wars have spurred some of the biggest inventions, which have had a huge impact on standards of living. If World War I served as a test bed for the development of the airplane and its use as a warcraft, World War II brought us the helicopter and digital electronic computer.

Manual and mechanical computing devices had existed since ancient times. From the abacus in about 500 BCE, there had been progress towards mechanical analogue computers in the medieval Islamic world in the 11th–12th centuries. Later, with the advent of electricity in the early 20th century, it became possible to develop electrically driven mechanical analogue computers. By 1912, Arthur Pollen, a leading British journalist and businessman, was able to produce one of the world's first electrically powered analogue computers, patented as the Argo Clock.

It was around this time that IBM was set up in the US. The earlier name of IBM was the Computing-Tabulating-Recording company (CTR) when it was set up in 1911 in Endicott, New York, as a holding company of manufacturers of record-keeping and measuring systems. It was later named as International Business Machines in 1924. It was IBM that supplied analogue computers to assist in the building of the first atom bomb, and later the first digital electronic computer was developed in the University of Pennsylvania and dedicated to the nation on 14 February 1946. Called ENIAC (short for Electronic Numerical Integrator and Computer), its development was necessitated by the need to calculate firing tables for artillery. It weighed 60,000 pounds, covered an area of 1,800 sq. ft. and had cost about $487,000, which was a phenomenal sum those days. After the war, ENIAC was mainly used to carry out calculations related to the production of the hydrogen bomb.

Following this, in early 1950s, there came a big push to the development of nuclear and space sciences, and consequently to digital electronic computers, as they were critical to their growth and advancement. Perhaps it would not have been possible for man to achieve the moon landing in 1969 had it not

> **Fun Fact**
> Climate Activist: Gates is deeply involved in tackling climate change, investing in sustainable energy technologies and advocating for policies aimed at reducing global carbon emissions.

Bill Gates and Paul Allen at Lakeside School in 1970
Credits: Bruce Burgess, Public domain, via Wikimedia Commons

been for the advancements in IT. Undeniably, most major human endeavours are marked by the desire to push the envelope. 'What next?' is the perpetual question.

In the late 1960s, a feeling had started growing in the industry as how to further improve and harness computer technology for the larger good of mankind. Scientists had even started wondering whether it was possible to put the computer on the desk to aid people in their day-to-day activities. As research was taking place in different areas of electronics, it was actually the advancement in the microprocessor technology that made this possible.

Microprocessor—the Game Changer

The radio of yore was a big bulky device that would occupy the whole table. Its big size was essentially on account of the large vacuum tubes that performed the function of controlling and relaying the electrical current. These tubes had existed since the beginning of the century, and were used in practically all electrical devices. Subsequent researches in the field, for an improvement on these, led to the invention of the transistor in 1948, which was a major step forward. However, what totally changed the electronic landscape was the integration of a large number of transistors

> **Fun Fact**
>
> Prolific Author: Gates has authored several influential books, such as "The Road Ahead" and "Business @ the Speed of Thought," providing valuable insights into technology, business, and future trends.

on a small flat metal piece (first geranium and later silicon), called the integrated circuit (ASIC, or simply IC).

Some early attempts were made in this direction around the late 1940s. In 1949, Werner Jacobi, a scientist working in Siemens, had filed for a patent for an early version of IC in 1949, which had only five transistors. It was a nascent idea that couldn't be fully implemented. More serious attempts were made in the late '50s with scientists like Jack Kilby, Robert Noyce, Kurt Lehovec, Jean Hoerni and some others taking the lead.

As there were conflicting claims as to who actually invented the IC and a patent war ensued, the American press later narrowed the list to Jack Kilby and Robert Noyce. Kilby was later awarded the Noble Prize in Physics in 2000 for his 'contribution to the development of IC.' The IC paved the way for the development of the microprocessor, which is the heart—the controlling unit—of a computer or machine. An IC forms the basis of a microprocessor that may contain more than one IC.

Over time, the convergence of technologies had continued to bring us more advanced and sophisticated products. So, when the scientists were able to integrate a large number of transistors on a single chip, it was considered a major breakthrough of the time; but as yet, few had realized the enormous possibilities it was about to open up for mankind. Another major fallout of these developments was that it became possible to produce chips on a mass scale, which meant lowering of cost.

Bill Gates signature.

The increasing powers of the microprocessor, and consequently its mass production, were set to change the entire landscape of technology, and in turn, the future of mankind. In time, microprocessor-backed technology would impact every field of human activity—from automobile to aviation, agriculture to education, medicine to nuclear, and space sciences to printing and publishing. Computerized devices would be found everywhere, ranging from people's homes to high-end nuclear facilities.

An overview of the progress of the microprocessor gives us an idea about its increased power and capability over time. While Intel's first-generation microprocessor, the 4004, had 2,300 transistors, the later versions continued to improve on the earlier ones, with the 8080 in 1974 having 6,000 transistors, the 8085 in 1976 with 6,500 transistors and so on. The Intel Pentium IV released in year 2000 contained 42 million transistors.

In short, with every passing year the companies have continued to make microprocessors faster and more powerful. The difference between the earlier and later versions is mainly the speed—the advanced microprocessors can perform millions of tasks per second, and quickly move data between various memory locations.

Thus, the stage was set for phenomenal growth in the computer industry, especially the PC (as it has a mass market). It was also the time for talent to seize the opportunity.

While young entrepreneurs with no previous experience but only passion and drive, like Bill Gates, Paul Allen, Steve Jobs and Michael Dell, had ventured out into the field, industry veterans like Gordon Moore and Robert Noyce of Intel also entered the market. This meant increasing competition. Intel was established in 1968,

> **Fun Fact**
>
> Book Recommendations: Gates frequently shares his book reviews and recommendations on his blog, Gates Notes, reflecting his passion for reading and continuous intellectual growth.

SAP in 1972, Microsoft in 1975, Apple in 1976, Oracle in 1977, Sun Microsystems and Adobe in 1982, and Dell and Cisco in 1984.

Front lobby entrance of Building 17, one of the largest on Microsoft's Main Campus in Redmond
Credits: Derrick Coetzee, Public domain, via Wikimedia Commons

Next Wave—the Internet

If the early '50s and '60s were the era of large computers and mainframes, and the late '70s a period marked by a growth in microcomputers and PCs, the early '90s saw a totally new dimension being added to the IT industry. A standalone computer is just a sophisticated typewriter, or a video or gaming device, but once connected to other computers, it assumes a different character and becomes a node in a large chain. Efforts were being made since the early '60s to produce some kind of network that would facilitate messaging and graphic and text transmission from one machine to another. The early attempts included projects like the Advanced Research Projects Agency Network (ARPANET), the NPL (short for National Physical Laboratory) Network, Telenet and others.

However, the real breakthrough came with the creation of the World Wide Web (WWW), developed by the British scientist Tim Berners-Lee, while conducting research at CERN Switzerland in the early '80s. This development made the linking of different computers possible, wherein the network could be accessible from any node. With its further development in the '90s, a new world—electronic messaging, voice mail, video interface, Internet—opened up like never before. If the railways and aviation were the major connectors for humanity earlier, the Internet has proved to be the next big thing.

The Internet involves interconnected software or hardware storage devices called servers, which contain all the content, web pages and sites uploaded onto them from time to time, and to which individual computers (or nodes) can get connected, share the data and services, and download or upload files. After the early '90s, the Net continued to grow exponentially, which meant more and more servers got linked to it, and millions of pages and sites got added to it.

> **Fun Fact**
> Avid Reader: Gates reads approximately 50 books annually, showcasing his dedication to continuous learning and intellectual growth, and frequently shares his recommendations and reviews.

Such was the environment in which computer companies had begun to vie with one another for a bigger and bigger share of the computer pie. One point to note here is, every individual (or entity) has his 'forte'; he can't be the master of all. So, interestingly, as the computer industry began to expand, there came to be a greater need of coordination and cooperation between the competing entities. If IBM was the big boy of hardware, it needed to buy the O/S from Microsoft; while Intel was the master of the computer chip, it needed Apple to drive its sale. So, while on one side they were competing in the market, on the other, they needed each other. Interdependence was the name of the game.

IBM head office Bangalore
Credits: Chinmayee Mishra, CC BY-SA 4.0 <https://creativecommons.org/licenses/by-sa/4.0>, via Wikimedia Commons

Hence, what began in the US in the '80s and '90s and gradually spread across the world, would, in the coming decades, become a race extremely exciting, and even unexpected at times. Some companies would be gobbled up by the bigger fish (IBM's purchase of Lotus), others might drop out of the contention (Hotmail selling off to Microsoft), while some others would continue to become bigger and bigger (Apple, Microsoft, IBM, Facebook, Amazon, etc.) and even get embroiled in monopoly issues.

4

Hits and Misses

> Your most unhappy customers are
> your greatest source of learning.
> —*Bill Gates*

Success and Growth of Microsoft

The fact that even after over four decades of fierce competition and 'tech wars', Microsoft continues to be one of the largest computer companies in the world has a lot to do with the drive and vision of one man: Bill Gates. It was the genius of Gates that could spot the opportunity, make the right move at the right time and turn things to his advantage. In other words, he had a finger on the pulse of the market and was able to offer a product that would have 'wide acceptance' and 'wide applicability'. Once the product was accepted by the people, he would ensure its repeat purchase, by dealing with the competition on one hand, and ensuring product improvement through constant enhancements and upgradations, on the other.

Till today, the Windows O/S and Microsoft Office remain some of the most sought-after programmes ever—and among the major revenue earners for the company. As they

> **Fun Fact**
>
> Think Week Ritual: Twice a year, Gates isolates himself for a "Think Week," a period of intense reading and reflection, emphasizing his commitment to deep thought and strategic planning.

Bill Gates at the World Economic Forum, 2007
Credits: World Economic Forum, CC BY-SA 2.0 <https://creativecommons.org/licenses/by-sa/2.0/>, via Wikimedia Commons

remain the company's 'jewels in the crown', the story of their growth and development calls for a comprehensive analysis, which takes us through the various developments and modifications they have gone through over time, and their current position therein.

However, looking at the general growth of the company, to begin with we need to focus on the period from 1975–95, as it remains the most important phase in the history of Microsoft. This was a period marked by success, growth and consolidation. During this time, the company had been able to establish its supremacy in certain areas and would remain practically unchallenged in those in the future. Although after the '90s, it kept making forays into other areas, like hardware, gaming consoles, artificial intelligence (AI), and later also cloud computing and PC hardware, for quite some time, upgradations and enhancements related to Windows and MS Office occupied the company's energies. It's only after 2000 that other products began to come into prominence. Since the first twenty-five years have remained the main foundation years, let's first examine this period in detail.

> **Fun Fact**
>
> Environmental Steward: Gates invests in clean energy projects, aiming to mitigate climate change and promote sustainable practices.

We know that after the success of MS-DOS in 1981, the company had got the resources to begin an era of expansion and consolidation. What further boosted the company's finances was the fact that IBM again approached them in 1985 for the development of an O/S for their next version. As was the case with the earlier MS-DOS (developed in 1981), this time again Microsoft continued to sell its own version of the new software in the market, which would later overshadow the IBM OS/2 and further improve Microsoft's revenue.

As the era of innovation had begun, one major feature introduced during this time was graphical user interface (GUI), which would become a permanent fixture of the PC environment. It was developed by Microsoft under the supervision of Bill Gates for Apple Computers and was later used in Windows 85. Apple took it to be an infringement of their patent rights, but later the matter was settled out of court. While earlier, the PC screen would only show the typed text, with the introduction of graphic icons, a certain richness and variety were added to the operation. It also freed the user from keyboard-command and allowed him to access files and data, using a mouse to click on 'graphic' icons. It was to be a new 'window' of experience for him—thus, the name stuck and later became a household name.

Starting 1985, MS-DOS, in the new avatar of Windows, with additional features like GUI, would be set on a course that would be unstoppable in the history of computers. From 1985 till now, about twenty-six Windows versions for the PC, besides others for servers and devices, have been released, the details of which have been discussed in a separate chapter.

Another major innovation during this period that improved the company's prospects in the long run was the development of Office applications—first Word, then Excel, and finally PowerPoint. To begin with, all these applications had been developed at different times, and continued to be sold as separate products. Word was released for DOS in 1983 and for

> **Fun Fact**
>
> Tech-Enhanced Home: Gates' residence, Xanadu 2.0, is a marvel of modern technology and luxury, equipped with advanced tech features and reflecting his interests and immense wealth.

Mac in 1985; Excel for Mac in 1985 and for Windows in 1987; and PowerPoint for Mac in 1987 and for Windows in 1990. Although they had been selling well individually and had good market share, it's only when their integration happened—first in a common package called Microsoft Office and later in the early '90s with the Windows—that the whole Windows package became an unbeatable product.

Around 1984, an IT magazine, *InfoWorld* (2 April 1984), had stated, Microsoft is widely recognized as the most influential company in (the) microcomputer software industry. Claiming more than a million installed MS-DOS machines, (the) founder and chairman... has decided to certify MS's jump on the rest of the industry by dominating applications, operating systems, peripherals, and most recently book publishing. Some insiders say MS is attempting to be the IBM of (the) software industry.

Growth beyond 1995

We're aware that right from the beginning, one of the biggest advantages of Microsoft had been the stupendous success of Windows. On the back of Windows, it could afford to experiment, innovate, expand, diversify and even take risks and afford to fail. Windows gave it the financial muscle to power its way ahead into the fiercely growing competitive market. In this respect, a rather unflattering term was developed by some writers, 'Embrace, Extend, Extinguish,' outlining Microsoft's general strategy of growth. The company would look for a fledgling product in the market, adopt it, change or modify it to suit its own needs and then make it its own, and 'extinguish' the earlier product. In a 2008 interview, Steve Ballmer, CEO Microsoft, said that the company's

> **Fun Fact**
> Business Strategy Influence: Gates' business strategies and practices are widely studied and emulated, highlighting his significant impact on modern business theory and corporate strategy.

policy was to continue to pursue 'new technologies even if initial attempts fail.' He gave the example of Windows, which Microsoft has continued to update and refine over time.

So, the growing revenue had opened up many new vistas of opportunities and possibilities for the company. It was able to hire new talent, invest in research and development, and enhance and expand its product range. As the company had already got a grip on the O/Ss and Office applications for PCs, its future policy was to follow a twin-fold objective: Firstly, not to loosen its grip on Windows and MS Office by ensuring complete customer satisfaction through upgradations and improvements, and secondly, compete with full might of technology and money power in other areas to get ahead.

Around 2000, the IT industry had started growing at an unprecedented rate on the back of a spurt in manufacturing and services activities round the globe—countries like China and India, with large markets, had started recording 7–8 per cent growth, becoming new engines of world growth. The fast pace of growth had necessitated the need for all kinds of IT products, ranging from computers to peripherals, custom software and servers to shared services facilities. The growth of the Internet was perhaps the biggest contributing factor to this increased demand.

One major positive fallout of the Internet was the general growth of email. It was believed around that time, that 80 per cent of the use of Internet was for emails. Microsoft's acquisition of Hotmail in 1997 for $500 million for those times was an expensive buy, but a strategic one. While the company kept on upgrading its Windows and Office offerings, it didn't lose sight of the general developments in the market. In 1995, Gates issued an 'Internet Tidal Wave Memo', which outlined the company's strategy in view of

Fun Fact

Innovation Advocate: Gates believes in the transformative power of innovation to solve global challenges, advocating for substantial investments in research and development to drive progress.

> **Fun Fact**
>
> Teen Entrepreneur: At 17, Gates launched Traf-O-Data, a venture aimed at creating reports for traffic engineers, demonstrating his early entrepreneurial spirit and technical skills.

the new developments in the IT field. It called for a renewed thrust in the networking and WWW space. Microsoft's MSN was originally intended to be a competitor to the Internet.

All this was in sync with Bill Gates's policy. He had always been alive to the market conditions, and the competitive threats arising therein. Although software was their strength, they wouldn't like to lag behind in the hardware and services areas. The company was among the first to introduce the GUI mouse with Windows. In the mid-90s when Internet entered the scene, Microsoft was quick to launch its own web browser, the Internet Explorer (IE). It had stiff competition in Netscape, but was able to deal with it smartly. In 1996, Microsoft collaborated with the National Broadcasting Company (NBC) to create a 24/7 cable news channel called MSNBC.

In view of all these developments, after 2000, Microsoft's thrust came to be in four main areas (apart from the Windows and MS Office products). These included the video-game consoles market, cloud computing services, mobile phones, and tablets and PCs branded as Surface.

Always interested in the video-game console market, Microsoft released Xbox in the end of 2001. The market, around that time, was dominated by Sony and Nintendo. Later, an improved version of the Xbox was released in November 2005 called Xbox360. The gaming console offered two versions: a basic version for $299.9 and a 'bells and whistles' version for $399.99.

> **Fun Fact**
>
> Research Supporter: Gates champions scientific research through various initiatives and funding programs, promoting innovation and the advancement of knowledge in multiple fields.

To deal with the growing IT services market competition, the Azure Services Platform was released on 27 October 2008, which heralded the company's entry into the cloud computing service market. It offers to clients on demand all kinds of IT services through the company-managed data centres. It was announced in October 2008, with the codename 'Project Red Dog', and was subsequently released in 2010 as Windows Azure. It later became Microsoft Azure in 2014. Given the competition and more and more players entering the arena, the company needed the extra push to make a place for itself. But over time, as its efforts have begun to pay off, it hopes to become a major player in the field in the coming time.

The next big step for Microsoft was the establishing of a chain of retail stores named Microsoft Store, to sell their products. The first store was opened in 2009 in Scottsdale in Arizona.

The launch of smartphones saw the company enter the market with its O/Ss. Although BlackBerry was a precursor to the 'smart phone', the device came into its own in 2007 with many improved versions, with LG introducing LG Prada, and later, Apple launching the iPhone. To begin with, Microsoft made determined efforts to capture the smartphone O/S market. It sought to revamp its aging mobile O/S, Windows mobile, and was able to replace it with Windows Phone O/S. To consolidate its position in the mobile market, it acquired Nokia's mobile unit in 2013 for $7 billion. In the PC and tablet market it made its entry by launching the Surface range of PCs in October 2012. For the company, it was a major event and shift in policy as its Surface range of PCs had hardware made by Microsoft itself, and was supported by Windows 8.

> **Fun Fact**
>
> Vaccine Proponent: Gates is a vocal advocate for vaccination, emphasizing its critical role in preventing infectious diseases and improving global health.

One important childhood lesson that Gates had learnt and which had become part of the company's philosophy was that one shouldn't be afraid to make mistakes; on the contrary, one should learn from them. Even if the company was not able to make much headway in one area, it was still worth trying. It would learn from the effort and plod on.

With respect to mobile phones and their O/S, and PC and tablet hardware, there had been much competition in the market and they remained Microsoft's weak areas. On 19 July 2013, the company stocks took a first major hit since 2000, due to the poor showing of both Windows 8 and the Surface tablet. Over $32 billion was wiped off Microsoft's market capitalization. Again, there was never very encouraging news on the mobile phone front. The company's share in the US smartphone market was a measly 2.7 per cent in January 2016. In early 2015, Microsoft had lost $7.6 billion owing to a drop in demand in its mobile business, and this led to the sacking of 7,800 employees.

> **Fun Fact**
> Infectious Disease Fighter: Gates' foundation targets infectious diseases, funding research and distribution of treatments to improve global health.

However, the good news for Microsoft is that in addition to Windows, which has been its strong point till now, Microsoft has been able to make its mark in new technology areas like cloud computing, Azure Services Platform and the gaming consoles business. In 2018, Azure's market share grew from 14 per cent to 16 per cent, while gaming product Xbox's revenue has been steadily growing, recording 39 per cent growth in 2018. The company has continued to explore newer avenues and expand in other areas. In a project named 'Azure Government,' it has partnered with seventeen American Intelligence agencies to develop products that track American citizens. It has also developed special equipment for the army, called the Microsoft HoloLens headsets, which enhance troops' capability to engage with the enemy by the high-power detection of their movements.

One business policy often followed by ambitious companies is, either develop a good product yourself, or buy a successful product and make it your own. That's the general trend the computer industry had been following beyond the '90s. As a consequence, many early competitors of Microsoft had disappeared as they were either bought by other larger companies or crushed by Microsoft itself. But then others kept showing up, keeping Microsoft on its toes. IBM bought Lotus in 1995 in an attempt to compete with Windows, and Oracle acquired Sun Microsystems in 2010 to strengthen its Unix-based software ecosystem. Novell was crushed by Microsoft in 1995.

Steve Jobs and Bill Gates during an interview by Walter Mossberg and Kara Swisher
Credits: Joi Ito from Inbamura, Japan, CC BY 2.0 <https://creativecommons.org/licenses/by/2.0>, via Wikimedia Commons

Mergers and Acquisitions

Ever since its public offering in 1986, Microsoft has, in all, acquired 225 companies, bought stakes in sixty-four, and has made twenty-five disinvestments. Of these acquisitions, 107 companies were based in the US. In its initial years, it made some major acquisitions that included Forethought, the creator of PowerPoint in 1987, and Hotmail in 1997 for $500 million. Some of its key acquisitions since then include: Flash Communications in 1997, NetGames in 2000, Visio Corporation in 1999 (for $1.3 billion), Nokia in 2013 (for $7.2 billion), Skype in 2011 (for $8.5 billion), GitHub in 2018 (for $7.5 billion), and LinkedIn in 2016 (for $28.1 billion).

In its 1989 financial report, the company had listed two types of competitors: In the software category, IBM, AT&T and Apple; and among the independent systems software vendors, Digital Research and AT&T. Although the company had made some forays into hardware by introducing the mouse with the 1983 MS-DOS, it was yet not a serious player in any of those categories, while the major competitors were vertically integrated. However, in its long journey of over four decades, the picture has changed considerably and today it presents quite a varied product profile after venturing out into new areas and through mergers and acquisitions. Though Windows and MS Office still continue to be Microsoft's major market strengths, its competitors have continued to change over time, and currently it has Apple, IBM, Amazon and Google as its main rivals.

5

Window(s) to Success

> I choose a lazy person to do a hard job—because a lazy person will find an easy way to do it.
> —Bill Gates

Windows & MS Office

As Windows and MS Office are Microsoft's major offerings, we need to analyse their growth and development in detail. First of all, let's look at the reasons for the success of Windows and MS Office. We know that Linux too had been in direct competition with Windows a few years later, and as it was 'open source' and thus free, it should've been preferred by users, but that didn't happen. Windows has remained the most popular choice among users.

According to Net Application, a tracking system, in July 2017, among the families of O/S, Windows had about 90 per cent market share, including all kinds of PCs in the world. One of the main reasons of its popularity is the 'ease of operation'—which means any beginner can operate it without much difficulty, with just some basic guidelines. In addition, it also offers advantages like backward integration, better

> **Fun Fact**
> Humanitarian initiatives: Gates has pledged to donate the majority of his wealth to charitable causes, highlighting his commitment to philanthropy and using his fortune to address global challenges.

driver support, compatibility with other versions, plug-and-play facility, support for new hardware and usage of a variety of software like photo editors, etc.

Given these advantages since its launch in 1985, it continues to be the most popular O/S for PCs. Starting 1985, MS-DOS, in the new avatar of Windows and with additional feature like GUI, had set on a course that would be unstoppable in computer history. Besides the twenty-six versions for PCs, and others for servers and devices, Windows is today available in 138 languages.

The company's objective all through has been to enhance and enrich the user experience. However, some versions proved to be highly successful, while some not so. Over time, the company has also discontinued support to some versions, while moving on to better alternatives. A closer analysis of this Windows journey would help to understand this progress.

The Many Versions

Despite many different versions introduced over time, many elements in Windows have remained constant. Windows 1 was launched in November 1985, under the supervision of Bill Gates, and ran on the original MS-DOS, heavily relying on a mouse, before it became really popular and an industry-standard. It was the company's first attempt at a GUI, which was to become a PC-fixture later. Because the mouse, as an input device, was a new feature, a game was introduced (Reversi) to help users become familiar with it, whereby they could click on icons using the mouse, rather than the keyboard.

Windows 2 was the next version introduced in 1987. It brought in new features allowing the 'maximizing' and 'minimizing' of windows, and

> **Fun Fact**
>
> Tech Visionary: Gates has a long history of accurately predicting technological trends, demonstrating his deep understanding of the tech industry's future and potential.

the facility of windows overlapping. It also introduced sophisticated keyboard shortcuts, expanded memory and launched the Control Panel, which has stayed till now. Microsoft Word and Excel too made their appearance for the first time with this version.

Windows 3, launched in 1990, offered improved design, higher memory power and better user-interface—and achieved broad commercial success selling two million copies in the first six months. It also required a hard drive. It was more successful than the earlier versions and challenged Apple's position in the market. It came pre-installed in Zenith computers. With 256 colours and multi-tasking, it made for an enriching user experience.

In 1992, Windows 3.1 came and it brought along True Type fonts, which, in a way, made it a viable publishing platform. The Minesweeper was introduced. It was the first Windows to be distributed on a compact disc (CD-ROM) and would be installed on the hard drive. With a facelift, it also offered a special version, 3.11, Windows for Workgroups, with integrating peer-to-peer networking bundled with it.

Windows 95 (referring to the year 1995) introduced the start button and concept of 'plug and play' to allow gaming, though this was not very successful. It introduced the task bar and for the first time, came embedded with IE. It introduced new features such as support for native 32-bit applications and long file names of up to 255 characters. It was extremely successful, and became practically a fixture on desktops around the world.

The next version in 1998 was built on Windows 95 and

How to Avoid a Climate Disaster: The Solutions We Have and the Breakthroughs We Need by Bill Gates

> **Fun Fact**
> Enduring Wealth: As of 2024, Gates' net worth exceeds $100 billion, reflecting his sustained success, strategic investments, and enduring influence in the tech and business worlds.

brought IE4, Outlook Express, Windows Address Book, Microsoft Chat, and NetShow Player, which was replaced by Media Player 6.2 in its second edition next year. It was a Windows Driver Model with support for USB (short for universal serial bus) composite devices, advanced configuration and power interface, hibernation, multi-monitor configurations and integration with IE4. It also introduced the navigation back-and-forth button and the address bar in Windows Explorer.

Windows ME, the millennium version, was the last Windows version to be based on MS-DOS. It sought to bring a blend between consumer features and the ones being aimed at the enterprise market being offered in Windows 2000. It offered some new concepts to consumers, such as automated system recovery tools, along with IE5.5, Media Player and Windows Movie Maker. As due to some basic flaws it failed to install properly and was buggy, it wasn't well received in the market.

This was followed by Windows 2000 in February 2000, which was the enterprise-twin of the ME version that later formed the basis of Windows XP. It aimed for the business segment, along with the domestic market. Features such as automatic updating and hibernation won it appreciation of the user.

Windows XP has been perhaps the most favoured edition of the Windows line. The company had been trying to enlarge the product's scope by including more enterprise features and it succeeded with Windows XP. Launched in October 2001, it brought both the enterprise mode and the consumer line under one roof. User-friendly elements such as Start Menu and Task Bar got a visual overhaul along with the introduction of other visual effects. Clear Types were introduced to make for easy reading on the liquid crystal display screen and the facility for CD burning was added to the features. With features such as autoplay for CDs, automatic updates and recovery tools, it scored over other editions. It became extremely popular and has had the longest successful run, with three major updates till April 2014, when it gave way for the next one. It was successfully running on 430 million PCs when discontinued.

Security remained an issue with this version as it would get turned off by default, and proved to be a boon for hackers. To counter this complaint, Bill Gates himself supervised the Trustworthy Computing Initiative with a number of elements and updates that would fortify it against attacks. In the market for six years, it was replaced by Windows Vista in January 2007. Despite all the research and innovation that had preceded it, Windows Vista was not able to make its mark in the market. To combat the security threat, the company had perhaps swung to the other extreme. It made the version app-heavy, requiring user account control and user permission to make changes—which was an outcome of Trustworthy Computing. This, in turn, made the operation slow and cumbersome. As many old PCs didn't run on Vista, it didn't quite make the cash register ring. Microsoft was even sued on account of its buggy operation. Media Player II and IE7 debuted on this. However, for gamers it included Media Direct X 10 technology. Anti-spyware, speed recognition, DVD (short for digital versatile disc) Maker and Photo Gallery were some of the new features introduced in this. It was the first Windows to be distributed on DVD. Later, a version with Media Player was created in response to antitrust investigations.

> **Fun Fact**
>
> Education Innovator: Gates supports innovative educational technologies and methods, striving to enhance learning experiences and outcomes.

Windows 7 was what Windows Vista should have been. The company's tech team had learnt from some of its mistakes and had come out with a winner. It made its appearance in October 2009. With a less 'dialogue-box overload,' it was crammed with many user-friendly features. It was faster, stable and easier to use. To address possible antitrust issues, it came with a pre-installed IE. A box allowing users to choose between different browsers was also introduced.

As the world had started moving towards touchscreen mode, Microsoft too decided to incorporate some of its elements. Windows 8 was launched in October 2012, and was radically different from the earlier version. It dispensed with the start menu and start button, and brought in touchscreen, with tiled interface icons replacing a list of programmes and icons. Faster than the previous version, it also supported quicker USB 3.0 devices. The Windows Store was introduced, and programmes could still be installed from other iterations of Windows. However, many users feeling more comfortable with the mouse and keyboard features

Bill Gates, Chairman of Microsoft Corporation, met Junichiro Koizumi, Prime Minister, at the Prime Minister's Official Residence in Chiyoda Ward, Tokyo Metropolis on June 29, 2005
Credits: Prime Minister's Office Homepage, CC BY 4.0 <https://creativecommons.org/licenses/by/4.0>, via Wikimedia Commons

didn't take to it. So, the company went back to the start button and mouse-and-keyboard operation in its Windows 8.1 version.

Windows 10 was released in 2015 and introduced many new features ranging from an updated start menu; Cortana, a virtual assistant for the desktop versions; Action Centre incorporating notifications and quick access to settings; a new web browser, Microsoft Edge; improved multitasking; and updated built-in apps. It has been well-received in the market and is likely to become the reigning Windows version. Beginning in 2015, so far seven major versions of Windows 10 have been released. The company announced that this was Windows's last version, and in future, the O/S would only be supported by updates.

Microsoft Word

From tablets to papyrus in ancient times, to typewriters and word processors in the modern age, humans have continued to look for more convenient and faster ways of written communication. In the late '70s, with advances in microprocessor technology and the emergence of the PC, there were ever newer attempts to produce a smarter and better word processor. With all kinds of scientists and experts making their forays into the field, by the '80s, there were about fifty different types of word processors in the market, offering different features and advantages. The most successful processor around this time was Wordstar, which offered automatic mail merging and controlled 25 per cent of the market.

Against this backdrop, Microsoft entered the market in 1983 with a word processor that ran, not on MS-DOS, but on Xenix. Xenix was a variation of Unix that Microsoft had earlier licenced from AT&T. It was released as a multi-tool Word for Xenix Systems. Over time, different versions were created to suit individual requirements of specific original equipment manufacturers (OEMs). So, between 1983 and 2019, there have been a variety of Word programmes; the major ones include: Versions for IBM (PC) on DOS in 1983, Apple ClassicMac OS in 1985, AT&T Unix

> **Fun Fact**
>
> Corporate Culture Influence: Gates' approach to corporate culture has influenced numerous tech companies, emphasizing innovation, competition, and a results-oriented mindset.

PC in 1985, Atari ST in 1988, OS/2 in 1989, MS Windows in 1989, SCO Unix in 1994, and Mac OS (formerly OSX) in 2001. With the growth in other technologies and products, different Word versions were also released for Android in April 2019 and iOS in May 2019.

In all, there have been about sixteen Word versions for Windows, fourteen for classic Macintosh and eight for MS-DOS, besides some others. With a view to upgrade its features and enhance user experience, it has continued to introduce ever new features—ranging from task pane, new XML-based file format, XML data bag, content control, and contextual tabs to file format 'docx', a ribbon-like feature to select page layouts and insert diagrams and images and faster shaping formats.

Modifications were also made to suit the touchscreen PCs and tablet models.

Microsoft Excel

Instead of filling each column and then making calculations at the bottom to reach the final result, one can use a few formulae by clicking a command here and there, and the entire table is filled correctly to the last decimal point—that's the beauty of an electronic spreadsheet, an indispensable tool in accounting today.

Accounting being the basis of economy, humans have been trying for better and smarter ways of bookkeeping since ages. Ever since the worksheet originated after the invention of paper, it had become the mainstay of basic accounting practices. Later, with the development of the computer, attempts were made to create an efficient and faster tool to this effect.

Actually, the word 'spreadsheet' conjures an image of a centrefold or a newspaper with both sides visible—corresponding entries in this case. In this respect, some initial work was done in the early '60s by Richard Mattessich, business economist and Emeritus Professor at the University of British Columbia. Later, the real breakthrough came with the development of LANPAR (short for LANguage for Programming Arrays at Random) by Rene K. Pardo and Remy Landau in 1970.

> **Fun Fact**
> Bridging the Digital Divide: Gates is passionate about increasing technology access for underserved communities, working to promote digital literacy and bridge the digital divide globally.

Although there was some dispute about patenting, the programme became the de facto system for a variety of calculations and tabulating activities. Soon, it came to be used by leading companies like Bell Canada and AT&T, besides eighteen other local and national telephone companies for their budgeting activities.

However, as work in this direction was going on in different quarters, one may say, the spreadsheet came into its own with the launch of Apple II in 1977. It incorporated a new spreadsheet, VisiCalc (short for Visible Calculator), developed by Bob Frankston and Dan Bricklin of Software Arts. Given the business applications of VisiCalc, it suddenly turned the microcomputer from a gaming device into a serious personal and business tool. It was regarded as a killer application and its sales shot up with a sale of 70,000 copies in the first six years, and over a million in its history. The popularity of Apple II prompted IBM to develop its first PC, and that's how other versions of the spreadsheet came into being.

New competitors that emerged on the scene were SuperCalc, Multiplan and later Lotus 1-2-3. SuperCalc came on the scene in 1981. It was an improvement on VisiCalc and thus got ahead in the market.

A year later, Microsoft introduced its Mutliplan, which was still a step ahead and was targeted towards systems running CP/M (short for Control Program for Microcomputers), MS-DOS, Xenix

Bill Gates
Credits: Jeff Sandquist, CC BY 2.0 <https://creativecommons.org/licenses/by/2.0>, via Wikimedia Commons

and many others. As competition was heating up around this time, the appearance of Lotus 1-2-3 changed the entire paradigm. It was developed by Lotus software in 1983, and sought IBM support.

Although IBM had a contractual agreement with the VisiCalc, and it was shipped simultaneously with the IBM-PC, IBM was inclined in its favour because of its obvious advantages. First, the name referred to a three-fold product use: it could be used as a spreadsheet, a graphics package and a database manager. As it got IBM support (like MS-DOS earlier) it was set to sway the market. Another novelty that Lotus introduced was a graph-maker that could make several types of graphs, including pie, bar graphic and line charts.

It began edging out all the other rivals and became the ruling product. Microsoft's Multiplan tried to cope with it but was not so successful. Although it sold over a million copies, it was being outsold, and in the mid-'80s and much of the '90s, Lotus had become the product of choice. In the market, people would ask for the 'Lotus PC'. According to Bill Gates, the main reason for Multiplan's lagging behind was that they had tried to align it with too many ports. In all, there were about a hundred different versions of Multiplan.

But Microsoft, with its competitive spirit, was not going to give up. While it was working on improving its Multiplan, Lotus began to run into rough weather. Microsoft released its improved version of Multiplan as Excel in 1985 for Apple Macintosh, which, for the first time, had a graphical interface. Later, in 1987, Excel 2.0 was released with Windows. During this time, Lotus had begun to suffer some technical issues in converting from a macro assembler to a more portable C language. As Excel was now part of Windows, which was a preferred O/S, its popularity soared. Lotus began to lose ground, and, over time, Excel became the dominant spreadsheet.

> **Fun Fact**
> Royal Recognition: In 2005, Queen Elizabeth II awarded Gates an honorary knighthood, recognizing his significant contributions to business, technology, and global philanthropy.

So far, over thirteen major versions of Microsoft Excel have been introduced in the market, each offering improved and upgraded features. From the early basic stage, it has gone on to induct features such as toolbars, drawing capabilities, outlining, multi-sheet workbooks, an interface for developers of Visual Basic for Applications, enhanced clipboard, pivot charts, model user forms, sparking graphics, pivot table slicers and single-document interface and charting enhancements.

Microsoft PowerPoint

A $14 million acquisition in 1987 has perhaps proved to be a bigger money spinner than most of Microsoft's products or other acquisitions. Initially sceptical about the purchase, Bill

Gates's acquisition today is installed on over a billion computers worldwide, and remains one of the most sought-after softwares.

First, some glimpses of business presentation devices and tools. Earlier, a business meeting meant the distribution of certain documents to the members, which would be followed by a discussion, with each member making his notes and speaking in turn. Over time, business houses graduated to chart presentations, and then slide projections when slide projectors came into vogue.

Companies such as Trollman, Genigraphics (a division of GE), Dicomed and others had devised computer workstations on which presentation graphics software could run a large number of slides. But then, it was an expensive and cumbersome process that only large corporations could afford.

In time, with the advent of microcomputers, especially the PCs, the whole game of business presentations underwent a dramatic

Ban Ki-moon, UN Secretary-General, and Bill Gates, Co-Chair of the Gates Foundation, at the 'Global Development Outlook' session, World Economic Forum, Davos, January 24, 2013
Credits: World Economic Forum from Cologny, Switzerland, CC BY-SA 2.0 <https://creativecommons.org/licenses/by-sa/2.0>, via Wikimedia Commons

change. So, in the early '80s, a large number of companies had begun to develop presentation software, and in 1987, Microsoft too had initiated its own project to this effect. But then, to speed up the project, the company started toying with the idea of an acquisition.

Out of the two options, Jeff Raikes of Microsoft preferred Presenter of Forethought because of its clear advantage of overhead presentations. Initially, Gates was a little unsure about the acquisition and had thought that the presentation application could be a feature of Word, and not a separate product in itself. In time, he got convinced otherwise and Forethought was acquired by Microsoft in July 1987.

To go back in time, Forethought had earlier initiated a project in 1984 with an aim to develop a presentation application for Apple Macintosh and Microsoft Windows. The work progressed satisfactorily and they were able to produce a major design specification document for Apple. On the positive outcome of this, Forethought was assured funding by Apple in January 1987. Later, in April 1987, Forethought was ready with PowerPoint 1.0 for Macintosh, and the first product run was of 10,000 units, which got lapped up by the market. Later, in July, the company was acquired by Microsoft. All through, the product was called 'Presenter', but was later named 'PowerPoint', as the name 'Presenter' had already been registered by someone else. Robert Gaskins, one of the two lead developers, called it 'PowerPoint' as it assured certain power to the individual presenter.

In mid-1988, a new version, PowerPoint 2.0, was released for Apple that went colour (from the earlier black and white) with thirty-five slides. Although initially received well in the market, PowerPoint was not able to acquire a desired share in view of many competing entities. One major reason for this was that as yet, the PowerPoint version for Windows had not been released and

> **Fun Fact**
> Art Enthusiast: Gates is an avid art collector, owning notable works such as Leonardo da Vinci's Codex Leicester, which reflects his deep appreciation for art and history.

Bill Gates presented his book to Naveen Patnaik
Credits: Government of Odisha, CC BY 4.0 <https://creativecommons.org/licenses/by/4.0>, via Wikimedia Commons

most of the PCs in the market ran on MS-DOS, which used the presentation software of Harvard Graphics and Lotus Freelance Plus.

It was only when the first version of PowerPoint 2.0 for Windows was marketed that the scene began to change. It was able to ride the popularity wave of Windows like many other products, took lead over Apple and never looked back. Since then, its worldwide market share has been estimated at 95 per cent.

Today, PowerPoint is available in 102 languages, including Arabic, Assamese, Bulgarian, Polish, Punjabi and Turkish. Compatible versions for Android and iOS have also been released.

6

The Next Chapter in Tech

> I really had a lot of dreams when I was a kid, and I think a great deal of that grew out of the fact that I had a chance to read a lot.
> —Bill Gates

Microsoft and New Technologies

In order to reduce its dependence on the Windows and Office products, Microsoft had begun to divert resources towards many other areas since the beginning. In some areas it found success while in some others, it was not able to make much headway. However, two segments where the company has performed impressively in recent times are cloud computing and AI. Let's have a closer look at the developments in these areas.

Azure Cloud Computing

First of all, what's cloud computing? In the beginning of the Internet, a lot of people would remark that 80 per cent use of the facility was for email. In time, it dawned on people that when you could send letters and pictures through email, why not big files and data? And thus was born the idea of cloud computing, which began to take concrete shape with Amazon releasing Elastic Compute Cloud in 2006. As the idea caught on, Microsoft saw in it a big opportunity and released Microsoft Azure in February 2010.

> **Fun Fact**
>
> Code Contributor: Gates personally reviewed and revised parts of the original Microsoft BASIC code, showcasing his deep technical expertise and hands-on approach to software development.

In fact, the facility offers a range of advantages to business houses. Before the Internet, they needed to have dedicated servers to store data and files. Now with the Cloud, any company can buy server-space in the network at a much reduced cost. So, no need of capital investment on server and maintenance and hiring of staff. The facility is not just limited to data storage or retrieval but a host of other technologies that individual companies wouldn't have been able to access earlier. As the service gives value, it's been catching on.

Today, Microsoft Azure offers a host of advantages to companies ranging from functions for server-less computing, virtual machine scale sets, service fabric for microservices and container orchestration, virtual network and content delivery network to traffic manager, file and disk storage, Azure-developed test labs, site recovery, container registry, SQL (Structured Query Language)-based databases and related tools, stream analytics, tools for developing artificial capabilities, a variety of machine learning, security centre, visual studio team services, resource manager, log analytics, automation and more.

Given its plus points, it today stands as one of the top vendors (and contenders) in the field, having earned a reputation as a 'highly reliable and secure public Cloud provider.' One of the main reasons for its surging ahead is the fact that a large number of networks round the globe are Windows-backed. And since Azure offers virtually seamless

> **Fun Fact**
>
> Tech Industry Pioneer: Gates' foresight and leadership in the tech industry have paved the way for numerous technological advancements and innovations.

connectivity, it's a service of choice. Above all, it offers a vibrant ecosystem by having collaborative arrangements with many other computer companies like Red Hat, Hewlett Packard, Adobe, Cisco and others.

Microsoft has been deliberately targeting government institutions, 'highlighting its security and compliance capabilities,' and its website claims that Azure has been recognized 'as the most trusted Cloud for US government institutions, including a FedRAMP high authorization that covers 118 Azure services.'

With Microsoft playing an aggressive player in the arena, Cloud wars seem to be hotting up. No wonder, Azure has begun to play catch up with the pioneer, Amazon Web Services. In an October 2018 report, it was stated that for the first time, Azure had beaten Amazon Web Services in revenue, recording $26.7 billion to Amazon's $23.4 billion in the past twelve months. With these rivals in neck-to-neck competition, IBM, also an early entrant, is today lagging behind. To counter this, IBM acquired Red Hat for $34 billion in October 2018, an acquisition that added $3 billion to the company's revenue annually.

> **Fun Fact**
>
> Education Advocate: The Gates Foundation invests heavily in improving U.S. education, aiming to enhance learning outcomes, promote educational equity, and support innovative teaching methods.

Satya Nadella, CEO, Microsoft, made the company's policy clear in this regard recently, 'Our Cloud platform and tools enable our customers to build tech intensity while ensuring we're addressing their tough questions around trust—both trust in technology and trust that they have a partner whose business model is aligned to their success.'

Clearly, Azure Cloud Computing seems to have a great future ahead, as it hopes to provide another security-net layer to the company like Windows has over time.

Artificial Intelligence

In the 18th–19th centuries, people would tie giant wings to their arms and try to fly from heights. Just as flying has always caught people's fancy, the idea of a machine-man has been equally fascinating—a walking, talking robot that would do your bidding. They say, writers imagine today and scientists confirm tomorrow. Writers, artists and film-makers have let their imagination fly in this direction since long. We have mention of Talos, a giant machine man in Greek mythology. The idea had continued to excite many a modern writer. Mary Shelley, a 19th-century writer, had come out with the story of a creature, Frankenstein, who, once created with the help of machines, goes out of human control and becomes a monster. In recent times, feature films using elements of AI, like *Star Trek; RoboCop; I, Robot; The Terminator* and *The Matrix* have been big box office draws.

While on one hand, scientists and researchers have continued to demonstrate the potential in the field, on the other, many

Dartmouth College campus 2007-06-23 Dartmouth Hall
Credits: Kane5187, Public domain, via Wikimedia Commons

people have also expressed their concerns about progress in AI. Stephen Hawking, the renowned scientist and astronomer, was quite apprehensive about the technology and had once said, 'The development of full artificial intelligence could spell the end of the human race…It [AI] would take off on its own, and re-design itself at an ever-increasing rate. Humans, who are limited by slow biological evolution, couldn't compete and would be superseded.'

But then, AI is one of the frontline sciences today, with large investments being made into it. We have factories in advanced countries where a large quantum of work is handled by robots. Robotics is also a discipline in universities and engineering institutes.

In retrospect, concrete progress in this direction was only made possible with the development of computers. Scientists began to think that if a computer can perform increasingly complex functions, why can it not develop independent thinking? And thus was born the concept of AI. Work on it had begun in right earnest at Dartmouth College, New Hampshire, US, in 1956. Scientists and engineers from some of the leading facilities such as Massachusetts Institute of Technology (MIT), Carnegie Mellon University (CMU) and IBM had begun working on such projects, and in a few years were able to report significant progress. Observers and the press called some of their achievements 'astonishing'. It was found that the computer could beat humans in standard tasks like solving certain mathematical problems and applying theorems, etc. They were even found to be playing board games like Checkers better than their human counterparts.

Encouraged by the success of these breakthroughs, the US Department of Defense, forever looking to beat the enemy, increased their funding and laboratories were set up all over the world. Herbert

Fun Fact

Enduring Legacy: Gates' legacy spans technology, business, health, and education, making a lasting impact on the world through his innovations and philanthropic efforts.

Alexander Simon, a leading economist and cognitive scientist, declared around that time, 'Machines will be capable, within twenty years, of doing any work a man can do.' Another leading authority in AI, Marvin Minsky agreed with him and said, 'Within a generation… the problem of creating Artificial Intelligence will substantially be solved.' However, the confidence these proponents of the discipline exuded at that time gradually began to wane as unexpected problems and hurdles were encountered. The government cut down on grants, and a long AI winter set in.

Windows 95 installation CD-ROM, which included the Microsoft Plus
Credits: Pedro Cambra, CC BY 2.0 <https://creativecommons.org/licenses/by/2.0>, via Wikimedia Commons

Research in this area was again revived in the '80s with the success of the expert system (a machine that emulates the human decision-making process), and with the launch of the Japanese fifth-generation computer. Although the AI market had reached over a billion dollars in 1985, some setbacks again slowed progress in this area. After the late '90s, a major push came in this area with the development of more powerful computers and advances in other fields. Today, we have robot-driven manufacturing facilities round the globe and intelligent machines in households like Siri, Alexa and Google Home.

What's Artificial Intelligence?

AI is the infusion of human characteristics into a machine. To take a common example, when we moved from the grinding stone to the electricity-operated mixer-grinder, it was a movement from manual to automatic. With one control, we can make a machine work day in and day out. With advancement in technology, man was looking at moving from automatic auto-rotation to a machine that, with minimal human supervision, would be able to take independent decisions and complete a task without mistakes.

So, just as we use our intelligence to do certain tasks, the machine too uses its 'artificial intelligence' to perform certain duties. Though both have limitations, machine intelligence has more of it. To understand the issue, it's important to see how the concept of AI has developed over time, how it is created and how it's becoming increasingly useful for humankind.

We know that, at the root, all computer calculations and performances are algorithms, which in other words, are a set of instructions to the computer, in a pre-set, rigid, coded format. In simple terms, the computer is told (by algorithms) that 2 + 2 = 4, and so, when asked a question to this effect, it gives the correct reply. Now, if a computer is allowed to modify its algorithms on its own, and is set free from the rigid format, make its own deductions and derivations through relative correlations, it enters the realm of AI. It might even offer you advice and guide your decisions. It's this switching from the pre-set mode to 'independent-decision mode' that infuses AI characteristics in a computer.

Now, for instance, the intelligent machine (Google Home, Siri or Alexa) knows that clouds are formed

> **Fun Fact**
>
> Early Tech Prodigy: At 13, Bill Gates wrote his first computer program, marking the beginning of his journey into technology and innovation. This early achievement set the stage for his future groundbreaking work in the tech industry.

by water vapours and bring rain, and if you're going out, it might advise you to 'take an umbrella or raincoat'. It has derived this conclusion on its own from a set of pre-existing algorithms fed into it. Or for that matter, the machine knows that you're a man of means, and also another set of information that 'gentlemen prefer blondes'; based on this, it might advise you against dating a 'redhead'. What the machine is doing is it's making its own derivations and deductions based on pre-existing information in its processing system.

Xbox-consol
Credits: Evan-Amos, Public domain, via Wikimedia Commons

Microsoft and AI

As is customary with Microsoft, it has always kept up with trends in the market. It had begun to make investments in AI early, and as time passed, continued to show deeper interest in it. One of its first major projects in this field was Kinetic, which used motion-sensing inputs to help users control and interact with the gaming console. The player would just use gestures and spoken commands with the webcam as an accessory to aid in operation, and without going for the gaming controller, to play the game. Initially, it was developed for Microsoft's video-gaming consoles, XboxOne and Xbox360.

Although gaming consoles continue to be extremely popular with users, somehow the Kinetic inputs didn't find much traction with players. But one positive fallout of this research has been that because of its low-cost advanced features, it has found application in many other fields, including the company's cloud computing platform Azure. Another major development in this field has been the use of simultaneous language-translations on Skype. Skype, which had facilitated communication over the Internet, had been acquired by Microsoft in 2010. Now with its AI add-ons, the simultaneous translation in many languages, including English, French, German, Chinese, Italian, Spanish and others, is available.

Although AI on its own may not be producing perceptible revenue to impact the company's books, its indirect role is being felt in every area of operation to improve its performance and productivity. It's making inroads in every field of human activity, whether easy or difficult, simple or complex. Aware of its growing importance, Microsoft set up its Artificial Intelligence and Research Group in 2016 with 5,000 computer scientists and engineers. The group has been making AI contributions in different areas, ranging from

> **Fun Fact**
> Healthcare Innovator: Gates' investments in healthcare span numerous companies and initiatives, driving innovation, improving global health outcomes, and addressing critical medical challenges.

language translators, gaming consoles, improving machine learning, examining the societal and individual impact of the spread of intelligent technologies and developing interactive tools (like Word Writer, etc.), innovative platforms for cyber-physical systems and robotics.

7

The Stumbling Blocks

> To win big, you sometimes have to take big risks.
> —*Bill Gates*

Flip Side of Growth

Growth has its downside too—on one hand, it makes you go with the flow to keep up with the momentum and sometimes even overstep the bounds of law; and on the other, your product's popularity can tempt others to produce duplicates and make you suffer revenue loss. In both cases, damage control is necessary to safeguard one's long-term interests. Bill Gates, in his journey through Microsoft, has experienced both kinds of scenarios—let's see how he coped with them.

Antitrust Case

The government's position in a free-market economy is that everyone has the complete liberty to grow, to maximize his potential—but no freedom can be unbridled. It's the government's duty to ensure a level-playing field for all. If with money or tech power, an entity tries to curb others' right to grow, or abuses its dominant status in any other way, it needs to be checked. This is the basis of the Sherman Antitrust Act, which was enacted by the US Government in 1890 to 'protect trade and commerce against unlawful restraints and monopolies.' The objective was to ensure a level-playing field and fair play for all—and the case against Microsoft was essentially seeking to uphold the spirit of this law.

Against this background, sometime in the early '90s, it came to the notice of authorities that because of its dominant position in the PC O/S market, Microsoft had been misusing its power in pressurizing its OEM customers into coercive deals. In 1992, the Federal Trade Commission began an independent inquiry to check if Microsoft was abusing its monopoly position over the PC O/S market.

As nothing substantive could be established, the inquiry resulted in a deadlock, with two commissioners on both sides voting for and against the move, and the inquiry was closed in 1993. However, in the same year, on 21 May, then US Attorney General Janet Reno took a suo moto cognizance of the case and began an inquiry on her own. In her inquiry, she found lapses and overstepping of the bounds of law by Microsoft. She also discovered that owing to its strong product in Windows O/S, the company had been subjecting customers to a variety of unfair deals.

> **Fun Fact**
>
> Renewable Energy Investor: Through Breakthrough Energy Ventures, Gates supports revolutionary renewable energy technologies, aiming to develop sustainable energy solutions and address climate change.

On 27 July 1994, the US Department of Justice (DoJ) put on record its findings, stating that between 1988 and 1994, Microsoft had abused its monopoly position in the PC software market by inducing many OEMs to pay a royalty for each computer it sold containing a particular microprocessor, irrespective of whether the computer sold was with Microsoft O/S or with some other O/S. For example, if a company sold one hundred computers but installed Windows on only sixty, it still had to pay a licence fee for hundred. This would naturally discourage PC manufacturers from using other O/Ss. In other words, it was a way to penalize the manufacturer for using a different product from Windows O/S.

> **Fun Fact**
>
> AI and Robotics Advocate: Gates promotes the ethical development and use of artificial intelligence and robotics, advocating for responsible innovation and addressing potential societal impacts.

As there was some other evidence too of wrongdoing on Microsoft's part, the DoJ made Microsoft adhere to certain conditions, whereby the company agreed not to tie other products with the sale of Windows. It was, however, free to incorporate them as additional features in the same software, if necessary. Among some others, it also put restrictions on the company to have more than a certain period of contract for sale.

However, the real problem for Microsoft was to begin later. It was after the arrival of the Internet that Microsoft was in for a major face-off with the government. In the beginning of the '90s, the IT industry was poised for a big change with the arrival of the Internet. It had introduced many new elements in the market that were to result in a major transformation of the industry and the general market on the whole. As the idea had begun to catch up, more and more servers were being linked and a large number of files and data were being uploaded to the Net.

Someone had remarked in the beginning of the Internet that it 'is the biggest library in the world, but all the books are on the floor.' So, along with the growth of the Internet, there was also an immediate need for an efficient browser that would help users access data available on the Net. So, there ensued a 'browser war' with different manufacturers competing to produce a better browser.

Browser War

The first major browser to hit the market was the NCSA (short for National Centre for Supercomputing Applications) Mosaic, which was released in September 1993. A graphical browser that was later ported to Apple Macintosh and Windows, it displayed images in line with the document's texts. It fired people's imagination and triggered a great interest in the Internet. Marc Andreessen, who was the leader for Mosaic, later quit NCSA and formed his own company, Netscape Communications Corporation. It released its flagship browser in October 1994, which was to take the market by storm, and create serious issues with Microsoft. It was one of the main reasons for the antitrust suit brought against the company.

> **Fun Fact**
> AI Ethics Advocate: Gates champions ethical AI development, focusing on creating responsible and beneficial applications for society.

Microsoft, which hadn't entered the fray yet, came out with its own browser, IE, in August 1995. Next year in 1996, while Netscape's share was 86 per cent, that of IE was only 10 per cent. To increase its share, Microsoft adopted its typical strategy to piggyback its browser on Windows. It began to bundle the IE with Windows, which meant it came free to Windows users. Since Windows was practically on every second PC, IE began to increase its market share exponentially. On the other hand, Netscape was a fine product, but unlike IE, had to be bought separately and took time to download, which was rather cumbersome. So, within four years of release, IE's share had reached 75 per cent, and by 1999, it had gone up to 99 per cent.

In view of these developments, an antitrust suit was brought against Microsoft by the DoJ and the Attorney Generals of twenty US states for using monopoly practices to illegally thwart competition by using its software dominance. The case began on 18 May 1998. It was argued that the company had forced PC makers to install IE along with its Windows system. The DoJ was represented by David Boies. The case, which lasted about one and a half years, saw Bill Gates's various testimonies and bitter arguments from both sides. A witness quoted a senior Microsoft employee as admitting to the company's intention to 'extinguish' and 'smother' rival Netscape and to 'cut off Netscape's air supply'.

> **Fun Fact**
>
> Productivity Guru: Known for his rigorous time management and productivity practices, Gates has achieved significant success in both his professional career and philanthropic endeavours.

In support of its claims, Microsoft presented many videotapes, but many of them were later found to be doctored. Gates was called 'evasive and nonresponsive' by a source present in the court. He argued over the definitions of words like 'compete', 'concern', 'ask' and 'we'. He repeated the expression, 'I don't recall,' so many times that it even made the judge chuckle. Microsoft argued that by such practices, the government was simply trying to prevent innovation and thwart the development of new products, under pressure from 'jealous' and incompetent companies.

On the whole, Microsoft was on a weak wicket, and the judge, Thomas Penfield Jackson, ruled against them (in two parts): On 3 April 2000, he indicted the company; and in June 2000, ordered a breakup of Microsoft as a 'remedy'. He ordered that the company be split into two parts: one to produce and manage the O/S and the other for software products. Microsoft appealed against the decision, and the Court of Appeals for the District of Columbia Circuit overturned Judge Jackson's ruling against Microsoft, and later, on 6 September 2001, the DoJ announced that it was not seeking the breakup of the company and would rather seek a lesser antitrust penalty. Microsoft agreed to settlements with PC manufacturers, with the assurance that a lot of their concerns would be addressed through different concessions.

During this time, an open letter was addressed to President Clinton by 240 leading economists, whereby they said that through many provisions of the Antitrust Act, the government was thwarting innovation and progress, and should avoid playing in the hands of inept companies. On the other side of the divide, critics of 'monopolistic practices' have continued to argue that companies such as Microsoft, which have become behemoths, would remain difficult to control much to the detriment of general welfare.

Anti-piracy

Piracy has always been a concern for Microsoft. Bill Gates got a taste of it rather early, when he had designed the first major programme for Altair. Although the product had become quite popular with computer enthusiasts, its popularity also proved to be a bane. Gates discovered that a pre-market copy had leaked into the community and was being copied and circulated in large numbers.

Gates had always held that talent and creativity could never flourish without the desired support and incentive. In February 1976, he wrote an open letter to hobbyists in MITS's in-house newsletter, in which he said, 'More than 90 per cent of users of MS Altair Basic had not paid Microsoft…And by doing so, Altair hobby market was in the danger of eliminating incentive for any professional developers to produce, distribute and market high-quality software.'

Bill Gates in the company of Joachim De Vos, CEO of Living Tomorrow, during the official opening
Credits: Kaatvrtg, CC BY-SA 4.0 <https://creativecommons.org/licenses/by-sa/4.0>, via Wikimedia Commons

It was the early days in 1993, when a trade journal in the US had reported that while the 'US has lost edge in the global manufacturing industry, it had gained in the computer software

> **Fun Fact**
>
> Netflix Star: Gates is featured in the Netflix documentary series "Inside Bill's Brain: Decoding Bill Gates," offering an in-depth look at his life, work, and thought processes.

business.' Around this time, the US had over 80 per cent market share of computer software in the world. But then, the journal also pointed towards an accompanying problem. According to general estimates, the US was losing about $2 billion annually on account of software piracy in the country alone—and five times in the rest of the world.

It was 1993 when the world PC market was at a nascent stage. Over time, the problem could still be handled in the US and the West through better surveillance methods and law enforcement, but was to become more acute in the coming time elsewhere. With the growth in the Chinese, Indian, South American and other markets of the world, it was set to assume alarming proportions.

Bill Gates receiving the Indira Gandhi Prize for Peace, Disarmament, and Development on behalf of the Gates Foundation from President Pratibha Patil at Rashtrapati Bhavan
Credits: President's Secretariat (GODL-India), GODL-India<https://data.gov.in/sites/default/files/Gazette _Notification_OGDL.pdf>, via Wikimedia Commons

Interestingly, in 2004, during a visit to China, Bill Gates was asked by a senior government official about Microsoft's income from China. When he mentioned a figure, the official was surprised and he asked the interpreter to double-check with Gates. In his view, the figure was too low. But it was correct. In China, the problem of software piracy was rampant, and it was estimated that about 90 per cent PCs ran on pirated software.

In November 2018, Steve Ballmer told Fox News that in China alone, Microsoft was losing to the tune of $10 billion due to piracy. The problem has been no better in India, another major market for PCs. At current prices, when pirated Windows software is available for ₹130, the original software costs around ₹9,000. The reality check is, while large corporations, on account of visibility and transparency, cannot afford to risk pirated software, individuals and small businesses escape the radar of surveillance and save on the expensive programme. In fact, in India, very often the hardware vendor himself would offer a free Windows copy along with the computer to boost his sale and retain the competitive edge. Why would the computer dealer lose his business? And who would peep into your house to see what kind of software you're using?

In view of the increasing problem, Microsoft has continued to deal with the issue in a variety of ways—ranging from online checks and offer of incentives and cost-cutting, to physical action with support of local law enforcement agencies. In 2009, the company launched its Windows Genuine Advantage, whereby it informed the user about the benefits of using genuine software, and outlined how it would provide better security and performance with regular updates. Despite the growth in the problem, it had become possible for the Microsoft team to detect the counterfeit software by detecting the IP address. In this case, the PC's background screen would go black and a message at the bottom would warn, 'You could be a victim of counterfeit software'. The user was urged to procure genuine software and get the benefits.

The company was supported by a lot of countries in its drive against the menace. In 2000, it was able to take legal action against

> **Fun Fact**
>
> Early Tech Investor: Gates was among the early investors in major tech companies like Apple and Google, demonstrating his foresight and ability to identify and support groundbreaking technologies.

piracy and illegal counterfeiting in twenty-two countries with the help of local authorities. In many countries like Argentina, Brazil, Canada, Colombia, Germany, Hong Kong, Peru, Poland, Philippines, China, Romania, the US and the UK, operations were carried to address the problem. It was reported in 2001, that over five million units of illegal software and hardware products of Microsoft were seized worldwide in the previous year.

In 2009, Mexican authorities conducted a massive raid with about 300 guards on an illegal operation in Los Reyes, a town in Mexico. In the operation, three people were arrested who had been duplicating Microsoft CDs, MS Office software and Xbox video games. Over fifty duplicating machines were also seized. In India again, there have been a number of raids by authorities in offices of some companies suspected of using counterfeit products.

8

'To Whom Much Is Given, Much Is Expected'

We have to find a way to make the aspects of capitalism that serve wealthier people serve poorer people as well.

—*Bill Gates*

Bill and Melinda Gates Foundation

If Bill Gates got his competitive spirit from his Protestant upbringing, he got his altruistic nature from his mother. Mary Maxwell Gates was a life-long community activist and also served on the Board of UWC. It was her firm belief that every individual must have some room in his life and heart for others—and especially, if you're blessed. 'To whom much is given (from him) much is expected'—this teaching was part of the Christian values inculcated among children at a young age. '(Mary) never stopped pressing me to do more for others,' Gates said in his Harvard commencement speech in 2007.

In 1991, his mother forced him to drive down from his vacation home to meet Warren Buffet. As

> **Fun Fact**
>
> Advisor Role: After stepping down from day-to-day operations at Microsoft, Gates continues to provide valuable insights and guidance as a technology advisor, influencing the company's strategic direction.

> **Fun Fact**
> Polio Eradication Campaigner: Gates has been instrumental in the global effort to eradicate polio, providing significant funding and advocacy.

Gates didn't think much of him, he was reluctant to meet him. 'Look, he just buys and sells pieces of paper,' said Gates. 'That's not real value-added. I don't think we'd have much in common.' But his meeting with Buffet proved to be the beginning of a lifelong association for both, and earned Bill another comrade-in-arms for a common cause.

Bill's mother was fortunate to see her son's wealth grow tremendously before her death from breast cancer in 1994. At that time, Gates was listed as one of the richest men in the world. His setting up of the foundation was, in a way, a personal tribute to his mother's memory.

In 1994, Gates had started the William H. Gates Foundation. Later, he and his wife combined three family foundations in 2000, and renamed them as Bill and Melinda Gates Foundation, to which Bill donated stock worth $5 billion. Its co-chair have been Bill Gates, Melinda Gates and William H. Gates Sr., with Susan Desmond-Hellman as the CEO. Today, it's the largest private endowment fund in the world with a holding of $50.7 billion.

Bill Gates in conversation with The Times of India
Credits: The Times of India, CC BY 3.0 <https://creativecommons.org/licenses/by/3.0>, via Wikimedia Commons

The basic objectives behind the foundation are: One, address healthcare issues in the world and reduce extreme poverty; and two, in the US, expand educational opportunities and improve access to IT.

During its twenty-year journey, it has traversed a long distance, achieving many a landmark through its fruitful endeavours. As on April 2014, the foundation came to be organized under five key functions:
1. Global Development Division
2. Global Health Division
3. United States Division
4. Global Policy and Advocacy Division
5. Global Growth and Opportunity Division

> **Fun Fact**
> Digital Literacy Promoter: Gates works tirelessly to increase digital literacy, ensuring underserved communities gain access to modern technology.

In June 2006, Warren Buffet, the owner of Berkshire Hathaway and then the richest man in the world with a net worth of $64 billion sought involvement in the Foundation and pledged to contribute on an annual basis a certain amount, with an offering of $1.5 billion in the first year.

Since its inception, the organization has been able to meet success on the various goals it had set out to achieve. One unique feature about the Foundation is its accent on transparency,

The Bill & Melinda Gates Foundation building
Credits: Sea Cow, CC BY-SA 4.0 <https://creativecommons.org/licenses/by-sa/4.0>, via Wikimedia Commons

> **Fun Fact**
>
> Controversial Business Tactics: Gates' competitive business practices have sparked antitrust lawsuits, highlighting the complex and sometimes controversial nature of his strategies and market dominance.

conspicuously absent in many other charities of the kind. It allows the benefactors to access information in respect to the areas where their money is being spent.

That aside, the Foundation has continued to earn laurels for outstanding work in poverty alleviation and assistance in the eradication of many infectious diseases. In 2005, Bill and Melinda Gates, along with musician Bono, were named Persons of the Year by *Time* magazine for their outstanding charitable work. In 2013, Hillary Clinton launched a partnership between the Bill and Melinda Gates Foundation and the Clinton Foundation for the gathering and study of data on women around the world. In 2007, the foundation was presented with the Indira Gandhi Peace Award by the then President of India, Pratibha Singh Patil, and in 2015, Bill and Melinda Gates jointly received India's third highest civil honour, Padma Bhushan. In 2016, then President of the US, Barack Obama conferred on Bill and Melinda Gates the Presidential Medal for Freedom for their philanthropic work.